Swimming in the Lake of Fire

Swimming in the Lake of Fire

Poems

Thomas Ronald Vaughan

RESOURCE *Publications* · Eugene, Oregon

SWIMMING IN THE LAKE OF FIRE
Poems

Copyright © 2020 Thomas Ronald Vaughan. All rights reserved. Except for brief quotations in critical publications or reviews, no part of this book may be reproduced in any manner without prior written permission from the publisher. Write: Permissions, Wipf and Stock Publishers, 199 W. 8th Ave., Suite 3, Eugene, OR 97401.

Resource Publications
An Imprint of Wipf and Stock Publishers
199 W. 8th Ave., Suite 3
Eugene, OR 97401

www.wipfandstock.com

PAPERBACK ISBN: 978-1-7252-7298-9
HARDCOVER ISBN: 978-1-7252-7297-2
EBOOK ISBN: 978-1-7252-7299-6

Manufactured in the U.S.A.   06/02/20

Contents

Acknowledgements | vii

A Romanoff Czar | 1
The Garden of Mr. Brown | 2
These Words | 3
Kissing Sylvia Plath | 4
South Alabama Morning | 5
A Hospital Call | 6
One | 7
Charley Fawcett | 8
The Sower | 9
Long-Fingered Witches | 10
Death At An Early Age | 11
Abraham | 12
The Discovery of
  Tranquilizers | 13
Phillip | 14
Rain Song | 15
Resignation | 16
John | 17
Cancan | 18
The Call | 19
The Poor Parishes
  of R. S. Thomas | 20
Socrates | 21
Over Hiroshima | 22
Watching Skaters | 23
The Message | 24

At The Red Sea | 25
Declaring His Intentions | 26
The Unsuccessful Surgery
  of Josef Mengele | 27
Lines to Christ | 28
Judas | 29
The Last Look | 30
Rain | 31
A Mighty Wind | 32
Wars I Did Not Fight | 33
Downed British Airmen | 34
The Clash of Arms | 35
The Deserter | 36
Lines For Shakespeare | 37
Moses Cannot Enter | 38
Coffee and My Youth | 39
Autumn Days | 40
For Nancy | 41
Visitors | 42
Ordering | 43
Ricochet | 44
The Pastor As Informer | 45
To Kurt Godel | 46
The Nun Prays to Mary | 47
Old Trains | 48
To A Man Killed In
  A May Storm | 49

Reading Thomas Merton | 50
Michael Servetus | 51
The Heart | 52
To A Woman With
    A Special Child | 53
Nehemiah | 54
The Sentinel | 55
A Funeral | 56
Communion | 57
For A Woman Who Refused
    to Leave Her Four Children
    Dying In A Fire | 58
The Notebooks of Leonardo
    Da Vinci | 59
Wounds | 60
Martin Luther | 61

Liaison | 62
Remembering | 63
Little Fingers, Little Toes | 64
The Scottsboro Boys | 65
The Waldensian | 66
Return | 67
Elegy | 68
They Have Their Reward | 69
Universalism | 70
What Fingers Cannot Hold | 71
In The Beginning . . . | 72
Swimming in the Lake
    of Fire | 73
Eskimo Survival | 74
At Nags Head | 75
To My Father | 76

Acknowledgements

SOME OF THESE POEMS have appeared in publications of the North Carolina Poetry Society, The Waldensian Museum, Third Lung Review, Synaesthesia, A SECOND CIRCLE IN THE DUST, I WORK OVER AT THE CUCKOO'S NEST, Cold Mountain Review.

A ROMANOFF CZAR

The revolvers blasted into oblivion the gentle man,
Shot to death because he would not learn what it meant to die.
In those bleak days a Czar was finding his earthy stature
And everyone was acting like a king.
So, what would I say to you now?
Better the bullets riddled your feeble body
Than you see Holy Russia crumble so fallibly, so completely.
You were not a man for those ungodly times.
Nicholas, may we, lesser and greater,
Learn what and what not to do.
In us all the peasant and the king:
In our hands the lethal weapon,
In our eyes the horror of the pistol's point.
And so we remember this:
Around the dead Czar's chair lay four,
Princesses once, princesses no more.

Czar Nicholas II, murdered with his family, 1918

THE GARDEN OF MR. BROWN

I asked about his dead wife
And he said, "Come see my garden."
Denial, I assured myself.
But if I tell this man
That he will not be well
Until he speaks of it,
He will surely say,
"Your ministry is over!"
He is that brash.
So we step to the garden gate and pause.
He opens both arms and shouts,
"To life! To life and all that lives!"
Is it a toast? Is it a hoax?
Is he denying everything we teach on Sunday?
His wet eyes turn to me imploring.
I do not care, and say with thunder voice,
"To life and all that lives!"
We stare at cabbages and peas and
Corn that droops its head.
He takes my hand and squeezes it:
"Thank you for coming."
I nod and walk away.
Today, I feel no need
To teach anyone
The proper way to grieve.

THESE WORDS

What are these words? They are of me.
What are the things you say?
That once upon a time ago
You thought you felt that way.

We each have other lives to live
In worlds and worlds apart.
But leave the secret safe with me—
I have a keeping heart.

KISSING SYLVIA PLATH

Your ponytail will bounce forever,
Your eyes will always say
That you are on the verge of something.
Reading your biographies,
We grow old and dull and cranky,
And resent being asked to choose
Between you and husband, Ted.
We will not!

But answer me this, and I am content:
In the weeks of your great poetry,
With your children asleep in their beds,
A pillow on the grating, deadly door,
Did you not know that thousands of us
Would have held you in our arms,
Kissed you softly,
And said, "Not now. Not this."
Would have whispered, to save you,
"Poems are never finished.
They are, like everything else,
Merely abandoned."

Sylvia Plath (1932–1963), American poet, died by suicide. Ted Hughes, (1930–1998), English poet, her husband

SOUTH ALABAMA MORNING

Twenty feet up
    Everything grays—
    Trees,
    Street Lights,
    Spanish moss,
    Haze.
It's 5 A. M.,
    Summer,
    Warm,
    Sexy.
I've just come down from
    Hattiesburg,
    Meridian,
And places further north.
Mobile invites me in.

A HOSPITAL CALL

With ease the grape slides down the surprised esophagus.
It will do him no good.
"How very thoughtful and considerate," said four times.
"How did you know I like grapes?" said three.
He is too young, early thirties.
He simply does not know what to say.
His range is narrowing.
The esophagus leads to inoperable carcinoma.

ONE

This place is hollow.
It creaks when I walk
And mocks when I talk to myself.
I have regressed in basic hygiene.
My manners are barbaric,
And how can one man disarrange so much?

Here, at a dinner of canned stew and tea
I write amid conspicuous absence.
It is insidious temptation
And I must not succumb:
You are simply away
And have taken my daughter.

CHARLEY FAWCETT

Quite bigamously and bogusly
Charley Fawcett married six women
In three months
To get them out of France.
On his way home
He was asked to smuggle microfilm,
Important to the Allied cause.
Charley was almost caught,
But he'd drawn some nude pictures,
And the giddy Nazis wanted them, too.
Charley slammed his briefcase in a huff,
Said in Southern drawl,
"Well, take them all .. .",
And walked across the border into Spain.
The lockstep lieutenant smiled,
Thinking he'd really gotten
Charley's Yankee goat.
Not a bad lifework
For a cunning expat,
Studying in Paris
Just before all Hell broke loose,
And several other Jewish girls
Were not so lucky.

Charles Fernley Fawcett (1915–2008), American wrestler, actor, model, resistance fighter.

THE SOWER
(after Jesse Stuart)

The soil is ready for the sower's seed.
He hears it beckon and takes timely heed.
The early days of April see him go
To test the odds that tell him it won't grow.
The faith that sends him to the fallow field
Is unexpressed but still believes the yield
Lies in the hands of One who's blessed before,
Years in the past, and will, he thinks, once more.
The sower lives close to the God of earth;
The subjects of his thought—life, death, rebirth.
No question of a resurrection proof,
For dead seeds live—affirmative of truth!

He senses in his heart earth's other call.
His faith remains. The seeds say, "Death's not all!"

Jesse Stuart (1906–1984), American poet, wrote "Man With a Bull-Tongue Plow"

LONG-FINGERED WITCHES

They are always reaching for someone.
As gnarled and knotted joints flex,
The raspy voice calls,
"Come here my pretty ones,"
Followed by a laugh which does not match.
There will be poking and rubbing and prodding,
All to determine the size of pot and heat of water.
Blackened teeth, warty nose, squinting eyes,
Framed by unkempt hair and fraying hat,
Almost complete the terror.
Add broom and candle, cave and cat,
And it is done.
The children tied firmly in wooden chairs
Wiggle and squirm and tug.
Through bulging eyes they watch,
They squeal, they smile.
This is all they have ever dreamed of,
And they have never been more delighted
In their lives.

DEATH AT AN EARLY AGE

If you have written songs,
    They will sing your songs.
If you have written poems,
    They will read your poems,
And be amazed in grief
    At your prolific verse.
If you have cherished ideas,
    They will cherish them, too,
In a process of creating you again,
    In a myth,
So they can talk of you still.
They will forget the negatives,
    And, in a human way,
Elevate your strengths to a place at which
    You will rightly be untouchable.
There, in that memorial,
    Ensconced among the stars,
You will, in time,
    Become fainter and fainter,
Until, when they speak of you
    Their eyes are dry,
    Their throats are clear,
And their words acknowledge
That your history is past.

ABRAHAM

The highest passion
> In the history of the world
> Is to still believe
> With all your heart
> That you will be
> The Father of Many Nations

While holding a knife
> To the neck

Of your only-begotten son.

After "Fear and Trembling," by Soren Kierkegaard (1813–1855), Danish writer

THE DISCOVERY OF TRANQUILIZERS

After an accumulated dose,
The wild beast,
Imago Dei,
Loses his scowl, piercing looks,
And terror of threat from others.
In weeks he is discharged to strange company
Of mother, wife, and son.
Seeing him leave, in our surprised minds,
We may choose to associate
"Also Sprach Zarathustra"
With this momentous exit.
We mark it well,
Not having been the same
Since we saw retraced before our very eyes
Part of the evolution of the species.

For some years I was on the staff at a large State Psychiatric Hospital, the setting for this and the following four poems.

PHILLIP

Phillip left for a Rest Home today.
He had told me things
He'd "never told before."
He'd seen the dead rise,
Amputees pull ropes with lost arms—
"Miracles! Miracles all!"
He came decades ago,
A rapist, hopelessly ill.
Nothing was "proved,"
But he stayed.
Now, at seventy-four,
We send him out
To socialize with the girls.

RAIN SONG

It is raining hard today.
Through the fog and cold
I hear the Music Therapist playing
"The Little Brown Church in the Vale."
The patients are shouting and singing.
It is an unusual chorus,
An unusual effort, this singing to God.
God and I sit listening
To the singing and the rain.
I have patients.
He has children.
Or so I choose to interpret it
From my office
On this cold, dark day in March.

RESIGNATION

A friend resigned and will leave us soon.
He has been troubled for months:
Depression and problems at home.
He knows he should not underestimate
This hospital's influence on his feelings.
Which comes first?
Which causes which?
Recently he has been angry and belittling.
We understand.
As a good clinician, he does, too.
We forgive him for this.
It is often the only way
We can say, "Good-bye."

JOHN

John is a volunteer, "here of his own accord."
He could not do much on Tuesday:
The voices came to plague him
Saying he should take his life.
Who is ever sure of such things?
They increased his medicine,
And that was that for then.
Some weeks later, stabilized and no longer
"Dangerous to himself or others,"
He signed out
And took a bus for Raleigh.
His father is there.
The voices and the suicides
Rode with him.

CANCAN

I do not think I knew
That legs could kick so high,
Nor skirts gyrate as if
They could begin to fly.

I know I did not know
That when a woman sits
She can smile as she does
Excruciating splits.

But I am sitting here
And I am learning fast,
And I am thinking of
The Parisian past.

Of what the painters saw
And what the writers heard
And how they played upon
This stage of the Absurd!

But what a stage it is,
And I can understand
How they could watch for years
Or even join the band!

And so I play along:
I sway and crane my neck,
Quite certain that I see
The young Toulouse-Lautrec.

So sure that I did not
Know what I thought I knew,
I swirl and kick my legs,
And wave at A. Camus.

Henri Toulouse-Lautrec (1864–1901), French painter; Albert Camus (1913–1960), French philosopher and writer

THE CALL

I hear another drummer.
I try to catch the beat.
But I cannot enliven
These slow and plodding feet.

And so I fall and stumble,
But cannot find my way,
As in the distance, fading,
I hear the drummer play.

THE POOR PARISHES OF R. S. THOMAS

Reverend Thomas willfully chose to associate
With those who sweat, smell, curse,
Have rotting teeth, use poor grammar,
And hold the world together.
They are real, he wrote, and we listened.
We know he spoke the truth.
Yet we cannot, for the life of us,
See why he continued this work,
Why he did not bask on B. B. C.
And take a college post.
It would have been easy.
It would have been so easy unless one were a poet.
A poet knows where he must be to write.
He moves in a world of ripe poems,
And they pluck him.

Ronald S. Thomas (1913–2000), Welsh priest and poet

SOCRATES

"I drink the poison in the cup!
I shout and sing—it is to life.
I use my hand, I lift it up.
I spin, and here's an end to strife."

And so they watched as Socrates
Unaided, saw his sentence through.
But history fell on its knees,
And Plato wept a tear or two.

Socrates (c. 470–399 BCE), Classical Greek philosopher

OVER HIROSHIMA

Perfect silence in the roaring of four enormous engines.
The sun seems a permanent light,
Fire and flame striking silver,
Crashing through clouds of a foam sea.
Earthmen encapsulated in an airless canopy fly.
Earthmen in unearthly suits poise on the edge of eternity,
Listening through wired ears for commandments.
"Target ahead. Bomb bays open," the wire says.
The precision men have no idea,
No concept of this deadly gift,
Nor will precision fail the atom gun.
The slow commandment comes: "Now. Bomb away."
Down, down, down, the thing descends,
Shaking lightly in the crystal air.
Faster, faster, as gravity exerts its pull.
Buildings, railroads, fields, grow larger in its eye.
Larger, larger, larger—
Catastrophe! Holocaust! Fire! Hell!
"On target! On target!" the unison relief.
On through space, as a dot against the sun,
Floating on the buoyant air,
B-29 swings softly toward a distant strip.
Under reflection of its shining wings
The mushroom cloud begins its slow expanse.
And unborn babes are weeping in their hands.

An atomic bomb was dropped on Hiroshima, Japan, August, 1945

WATCHING SKATERS

From your wheelchair
You watch the skaters' delight.
The ice is cold
And their breath is white.

But you are not here,
And you are not skating.
These are not the achievements for which you yearn.
You have not set your heart
On a double turn or a crisp Salchow.

You have, rather, with purity of heart,
Wished only to awaken
Without need to call the impatient mother,
To turn through the power of wholeness,
Sit up straight, clean,
And place two feeling feet upon the floor.

Do not be diverted by these flowing forms,
Liquid and lucid on a background of white.
Their skill presupposes the mastery you seek,
But cannot consider your single pain.
They have simply forgotten
What you never can nor could.
The human condition, is it not?

From your wheelchair
You watch the skaters' delight.
The ice is cold
And your breath is white.

THE MESSAGE

And say, please say, she understood,
And that she was surprised.
And say she was affected for
You saw it in her eyes.

And say she turned and looked away
And stared a long time there,
And that a wistful smile appeared
Before it thinned to air.

A life, my life, a lifetime now
Is gone, but who will say
That choices made so long ago
Can ever stay away?

AT THE RED SEA

Some bodies wash ashore, some bob like corks.
The water gives them movement, and they move,
Impressive in their leather, with their swords,
Stern helmets and the shields that pull them down.
And horses, too—it is a sight to see—
Not running in the field or by a lake,
Their musculature tense, soft flowing mane,
Long swishing tails now sweeping at the sand.
A crowd is lining up to watch and stare.
Some count, some weep, some laugh hysterically.
A man begins to sing, and all join in;
They seem to know the music and the words.
Their ancient anthem ripples on the waves:
"O executing water, hear us praise!
Should Yahweh rend the skies and come right now,
He would be lovely, lovely in our eyes."
And what a fierce theology they spin.
They do not take offense, no questions ask:
God merely took an angry king to task.
A child loosens a wheel that would not move,
And rolls it to a friend; they run to play.
Young girls with misting eyes look to the sea.
They smack their tambourines and start to sway.

Red Sea, Old Testament story

DECLARING HIS INTENTIONS

Between her blushing commas
He inserted only words,
And looks that told
Where lips and hands would explore
With her permission.
He had wondered at the proper order:
Words or actions first?
But as the product of the Age of Psychology,
He spoke.
Expressing appreciation for his admiration,
She chose another psychology,
Blushed again to say, "Yes".
Then reminded him with words
That they had been married for twenty-five years.
But he had not forgotten,
And said, "Behold, all things are new!"

THE UNSUCCESSFUL SURGERY OF JOSEF MENGELE

One day Mengele took identical twins
Into his discovery room,
And just to prove he could,
He, along with highly-trained staff,
Made them Siamese.
After recovery they were roughly returned
To anxious parents.
In their unrelieved horror,
The girls could, of course,
Only lie still and whimper.
But after dark,
In the silent splinter bins,
The Hungarian peasants mustered all their love,
And, while mother gasped,
Father smothered them into singular peace.

Years later, in the lush coffee jungles,
Mengele amazed even himself
Discoursing with friends
About the vast possibilities
Inherent in the Master Race.

Josef Mengele (1911–1979), notorious Nazi concentration camp physician, escaped to South America

LINES TO CHRIST

Fire came to earth in starlight
Born again to life the man
More was done by Jesus' sword tongue
Than was done by sword in hand

Wandered lonely for a season
Passed the fishermen, the sea
Raised his voice to God in anguish
God spoke through him, "Follow me"

Lightning struck Judea's hillsides
Magnetized the wind and sand
Fireballs of goodness marvelled
Seeing sick eyes, useful hands

Sandaled feet he moved more quickly
More often the doom he sensed
Silenced he defied a king
With words he stirred six continents

JUDAS

See man run.
    His sandals puff the dust.
    His clothes fly in the air.
    He is fleet afoot
Running from himself
To his own propitiation.
    The rope will choke his sin
    But there is no forgiveness.
He runs to the wrong tree.

THE LAST LOOK

The old man sits in the front porch swing.
His wet stubble chin dampens the khaki shirt.
Before him roll the thousand yesterdays
Like a dim film, a long hallucination.
He mumbles back into being
The times of hard work,
Better than any man's,
Days of children who grew up
To love him and to take him in,
Nights of the pricey women,
Before and after marriage,
Women he met once and only once.
He sees another man in another time
Doing the impossible things of today.

The never-wed daughter shatters his dream
With a call for dinner and an early nap.
He rises from the swing, surveys the land,
And shuffles to the door of this large house.
He turns and looks again.
Across the fields of his aging mind
The children are running in their glory.

RAIN

It rains on mighty oceans,
And in the seven seas.
It rains on winding rivers,
But never matter these.

It rained the day she told him
He could not have her hand.
And it will rain forever
And chill one heart of man.

A MIGHTY WIND

A mighty wind was blowing,
The wildest we had heard.
We held each other closely
And did not speak a word.

The evening passed so slowly,
The night ticked down to day.
We walked out on a world to see
Our fears had blown away.

WARS I DID NOT FIGHT

I lived through wars I did not fight,
Where better men laid down their lives.
I gloried in their victories,
And rent my heart amid their cries.

In brave, objective distance I
Have marched with them, and not for nought.
And I have died a thousand times
Alone, in wars I never fought.

And this my paltry praise to them
Who gave their all but did not, yet,
Enjoy this future won in wars
I never fought, nor can forget.

DOWNED BRITISH AIRMEN

Hurricane pilots with scarred faces
Would go to town in groups for drinks.
Sometimes women would come over
And give them a passionate kiss.
Sometimes they would stay the night.

After the war, no doubt, the women
Got married, had babies, drove cars.
I have always wanted to erect
A monument to them,
The base of which would read,
"It is a glorious thing
To kiss a burned airman for your country."

Years later, the men would look up
At the brilliant English sky,
And someone, for a practical joke, would yell:
"Jerry's up! Jerry's up! Scramble!"
The hard, thick lips would smile,
For they knew Jerry was down forever.

Yet, I think that sometimes in that sky
They could see the fighters fight,
The machine guns spit, could hear
The noise become a spinning din.
And sometimes a beautiful woman
Would suddenly turn her head,
See everything, too, and walk over
With a different fire.

I do not know, but that is what
I think happened often to the old Hurricane pilots
After the Messerschmidts hit,
Engines exploded,
And the hellish flames melted
Their bright and handsome faces.

Hurricanes and Messerschmidts, Allied and German planes of the Battle of Britain, 1940

THE CLASH OF ARMS

The clash of arms can kill.
All men know it is so.
They know it from their birth—
Life is the treasured worth—
But still they arm and go.

And just before the fight
Or after it is won,
Or after it is lost,
And many paid the cost,
They then lay down alone.

In sad and ancient lore
When kings went out to fight
Some senseless, urgent war,
Upon some windswept shore,
They dreaded most the night.

How do you rest at eve
When earth is cold as stone,
Beside a thousand slain,
When nothing will remain,
And nothing can atone?

THE DESERTER

If I could write in diamonds
The names across the sky
Of those who stood and stalwart
While others fled, and I
Joined with the band of shirkers
And would not stay to fight,
Then sun-refracting diamonds
Would prism-forth the light,
And there would be no night.

LINES FOR SHAKESPEARE

Language worked on with a surgeon's skill.
The intricate diction, precise analogy, perfect phrase,
All wrung from lips of the exact character.
Worlds revolved around that great head,
Pierced the brain with such succession
That all ages doubted.
He did not.
His mind was theirs,
And they came, ever came,
Walking, displaying, conversing,
Acting out their lines.
Acknowledging their presence,
He took his pen and wrote.
Spirit after spirit reviewed the work,
Approved, then vanished forever.
Through the darkness
The sonnets came for light.

William Shakespeare (1564–1616), regarded the greatest writer in the English language

MOSES CANNOT ENTER

There is the land you murmured for,
You bleated like sheep for.
Take it! Take it all!
Kill its warriors and their sweaty women.
Bring down the fire of heaven upon them.
It is yours, do you hear! It is yours!

I have stood in my ecstasy
And seen those arid spaces burst with water.
I have seen those oases which will sup you well.
Those fields will yield to your hands,
The women to your prolific seed.
There is the land! There is the Promise.

I, Moses, took you through the furnace and the dry throats.
I whipped you through the whimpering days.
I beat your soul like a dog.
And here you are at the gates of your destiny,
In this faithless daze.

Well, off. Away, my weary camp!
Lift your heavy feet and rumble
Toward I know not what next.
It has been spoken that I must stop here
And grapple alone with my final hour
In this barren and frightening context.

Moses' death, Exodus 34

COFFEE AND MY YOUTH

The old black pot sat on the black wood stove.
Granddaddy's cup was twice as big as mine.
I'd watch him and he'd watch me.
And we'd eat eggs fried, ham fried,
And big-size biscuits one by one.
He'd smile as only he could smile,
And with every bite his false teeth clicked.

Between big, healthy bites we'd drink strong coffee—
His black and plain but mine creamed and sugared good.
One cup for me, but his second was a sight.
He'd pour it slowly into the saucer,
Raise it to his mouth,
Blow it cool, and slurp.
Boy, that coffee was good, saucer after big saucer.
He'd smile in his onionskin baldness
As no one else could smile.

Even then I knew I was being treated to something rare.
Since I would not do it in my age,
It would die in his.
When his heart stopped, the old truck ran
Into a field and stalled out.
They found him slumped over the steering wheel.

AUTUMN DAYS

The autumn comes with autumn days
And autumn is my lot.
For spring and summer both are gone,
And this has Time begot.

But even if the seasons change
And shorter days unfurl,
Still I must take my challenge up
And walk out in the world.

For others are in winter chill.
This life has not been kind.
And some have not found springtime bright—
And is their pain not mine?

So all around and everywhere
If one can chain regret,
A man who has his autumn strength
May make a difference yet.

The autumn comes with autumn days
And leaves are falling fast.
And it is now or never that
I do the things which last.

FOR NANCY

We visit.
    We slip.
    We speak of baldness and you are bald.
It is inadvertent,
And you forgive us.
    Without speaking a word
    You tell us to share your comfort
With a body full of death,
And not to fear,
    As you do not,
The dark stranger
    Who will come
    Any day now,
And take you away from us forever.

VISITORS

Helping those people pack
Is somewhat of a relief
Because, even though they are family,
They're the kind of people
Who make you worry about your house,
And whether your stomach pooches,
And if your hair looks thin.
So you don't feel sad at all
Waving goodbye as they drive off smiling,
With a box of Peanut Brittle
On the dash.

ORDERING

In old age
    We should be ordering
Not verbs or nouns
Or adverbs,
Not lines or hair
    (I wish I could.)
In old age I think
We should be ordering
And straightening
    And tidying up
Our adjectives.

RICOCHET

To scare the hungry thing away
I shot into the sky.
But sometimes bullets ricochet
And innocents can die.

So long I stood and looked upon
The thing I had destroyed,
Then dug a grave and placed it there,
My resolution buoyed

To nevermore act foolishly
Or angrily repair,
Since I now knew that deadly things
Return when launched in air.

I raised my face toward the sun
To seal the vow I'd willed,
Then felt a burning in my breast
And all my world was stilled.

And as another man began
To lay me in the ground,
He wept to make his conscience clean:
I watched without a sound.

THE PASTOR AS INFORMER

"Oh, he's finally given up, I believe.
No more hope for him."
(But on the bridge the hands that grasp the rail
Feel more than steel, feel hope.)
"Even so, we've done all we can.
The family and all, you'll tell them?"
(But in the alley the fingers that push the plastic
Feel more than fear, feel life.)

Pushing through my veins the unctuous strength,
The fluid of soothing vocabulary,
Crawling through my brain
The confidence that will allow me
To walk through that door
And say in tender, winsome, pious words,
"Your child is dead," as if someone somewhere
Could add it all up and say,
"We finished in the black!"
At that bed was needed addiction and suicide.
I tried both, but neither wanted more, nor died.

TO KURT GODEL

I want to say something religious to you,
To point us both away from ourselves.

Above every all-encompassing system
There is another perspective,
Another mental perch from which we say
That such and such is complete,
Or, that such and such fails here.
You showed me another way to speak of God.

When logics die
It is residual man
Who has made that discovery.

Godel (1906–1978), mathematician, philosopher, developed The Theory of Incompleteness

THE NUN PRAYS TO MARY

O Mother, Mother of me,
A dark wind blows foul, foul.
A rough wind in the trees
Shakes and rakes and drives things on.

O Mother, Mother of me,
A black cloud runs pain, pain.
A dark cloud in the sky
Rumbles and rushes and pushes things on.

O Mother, dearest Mother,
A cold rain drops evil, evil.
A long rain in the air
Drinches and rinses and floods thing on.

O Mother, Holy Mother,
A warm light breaks mercy, mercy.
A thin light in the heart
Eases and teases and lightens things on.

O Mother, Mother of me,
A soft love gives glory, glory.
A deep love in the soul
Stresses, caresses, and blesses things on.

OLD TRAINS

The trains I used to ride
Are all gone to decay
In yards beyond the towns
And safely out of way.

But often in a glance
Or scene that takes me back,
I am aboard once more
With engine and with track.

I travel north or south,
I travel all alone,
To parent here or there.
I am not going home.

For home was in a time
And place I long since lost.
So trains began to run
And children paid the cost.

The trains are far away,
No more the engine cry.
But still a man can sit
And watch old trains go by.

TO A MAN KILLED IN A MAY STORM

Your plows broke God's ground day in and day out.
You were seen among the long fields by day and by late night,
Known among the ridges, hills, ponds, and lakes.
You told me once you had no choice,
That your lot was cast in that earth.
And so, despite the economics and statuses of those urban days,
You strolled, solitary in the distance,
To see what things shot forth.

That day you were creasing the wet sod,
Your tractor spitting and coughing against turbulent wind,
When somewhere over your rain-soaked cap
The mighty charge grew restless
And cracked through the damp air.
I have no doubt that under your caked wheels
God's gray ground will grow green,
That when He says, "Son, work in my vineyard,"
You will reply, "Sir, I go," and go.

Cf. Matthew 21:28

READING THOMAS MERTON

Looking Christ-like, hair blown in the wind,
The young man cleans the windows of my small office,
Holding me in cautious respect as I sit reading
"The Selected Poems" of Thomas Merton.
I imagine his contempt as he notices the title.
I sense revulsion: "Poetry, O my God!"
Yesterday, I overheard his conversation
Of buying a new car, a hot rod, and all the girls.
He has surely left behind forever
The poems, formulas, theories,
Experiments, assignments, and papers.
Somewhere, in the dim, unrecollected past,
We made a transition that ensured this sudden exchange.
I read poems; he washes windows.
In his contentment my envy flares.
I return to my reading:
The monks are milking cows,
Reaping wheat, sawing wood—Happy!

Thomas Merton (1915–1968), American poet and Trappist monk

MICHAEL SERVETUS

On his way to the stake
    he turned and saw Calvin
    and his flowing beard
    and his armour
    and the will of God
    and the inevitability of it all.

What he did not see
    was the young man
    with the bird in his hand
    to crush or set free.
Or the child held upside down
    with a sword between his legs
    and a screaming mother
    and a stubborn mother.

As the torches dropped
Calvin gloated and clucked.
Servetus shook his head
    and called upon the one true God,
    stunned to a daze
    by the psychopathology of dogma.

Servetus (1511–1553) burned at the stake, condemned by John Calvin (1509–1564)

THE HEART

Now clutch your heart with both hands
For love is skipping by.
Turn your head and glance away—
Do not look eye to eye.

I know that it is tempting
To give the thing away.
But you will come to thank me
Upon a wiser day.

You see, the heart is tender
And lies long in the breast,
And it is meant to stay there
For there it beats the best.

So none the hands should hold it,
And fewer but your own.
You will not soon regret it—
Let love go on alone.

TO A WOMAN WITH A SPECIAL CHILD

I see the children laughing, and my penance begins.
I think of my ruthless impatience, my dagger words.
What informs your resolution?
How have you walked that stage these fifteen years?
I see the children smiling.
I see the hearing aids,
I see the dark, sunken eyes.
He cannot be the child of night's hot love.
As you take his arm and stumble-walk from this place,
I throw you my wreath, my hand kiss, my crown.
I am crushed that my splendid, bleeding heart
Can do no more for you.

NEHEMIAH

When bricks and mortar fall
Before you on the ground,
Rebuild, young man, rebuild.
And make the building sound.

Take trowel in one hand,
The other touch the sword.
Rebuild the temple walls
And house to house the Lord.

And when the work is done
And tools are put away,
Lift high the sharpened sword
Then fall to earth and pray.

If bricks and mortar fall
Before you on the ground,
You can rebuild, young man—
The building will be sound.

Old Testament story, Book of Nehemiah

THE SENTINEL

Not to be taken by surprise
Is sure the best defense.
To stately stand as sentinel
While guarding every sense.

Of which, I'm told, there must be five,
And one of them is sight.
But it is soon so compromised
By visions in the night.

If one be lost, that leaves but four,
And one of them is touch.
But flesh begins where velvet ends,
Where hands and fingers clutch.

If two be gone, there still are three,
And one of them is smell.
But breathing deep while closing eyes
Cannot be guarding well.

So three are done, and two remain,
And one of them craves sound,
Which heard so close, so temptingly,
Once lost cannot be found.

And so to keep the heart secure
Remains undaunted taste.
But lips are soldiers in reserve
And never can be chaste.

Yes, every now and then again
Strong walls come crashing down.
And armoured hearts, though insecure,
Rise up and look around.

And when the senses reel and fall,
Preserving what they can,
Where once a mighty guardian stood
A trembling lover stands.

A FUNERAL

She knew only one man's hands,
Only one man's love.
He told me she had never kissed another man!
They were married sixty-one years.
She brought forth children,
Three boys and three girls.
No boy lived out of adolescence,
So he said his good name would die.
        At the end
Of all the gatherings and summings up,
Materially, they had nothing—
Nothing but a love that transcended their plight
And cemented them together forever.
        He has memories enough
For all his remaining days.
I feel no sorrow, absolutely none,
As I commit her body to the ground.

COMMUNION

The Great Invitation extended,
    I come.
The aisle is long
    And my eyes angle upward
    To the Cross of wood.
We gather.
I break this bread with those I do not love.
With those I do not love I share this cup.
God comes and stirs my troubled soul again:
    This bread!
    This wine!
My heart the Lord lifts up!

FOR A WOMAN WHO REFUSED TO LEAVE HER FOUR CHILDREN DYING IN A FIRE

The flames were ingesting them.
Even the screams were charring.

Time for decision was brief.
You chose quickly,
Walked into the wall of fire,
Made no utterance
As you took the hot shroud.

Yours was the silent joy
Of knowing your mothering was unaccomplished
And you were certain it was not to end.

Inspired by an actual incident

THE NOTEBOOKS OF LEONARDO DA VINCI

A dot below the nose,
Centered between the nose and upper lip,
Is the point from which life's vectors launch.
We intend outward by speaking and seeing,
And find the locus of life between these two.
This dot at the cup of the lip
Balances the forces:
Feet are far below,
The brain a decimeter behind and above.

If we draw lines at strategic points
Through an erect anatomy,
We are surprised by the perfect lucidity of the coordinates,
And such a form in motion is at once
Geometric, poetic, and silently musical.

Leonardo da Vinci (1452–1519), Renaissance polymath

WOUNDS

From self-inflicted wounds
There is no blood to show,
For psyches do not bleed
Despite how deep they go.

But not to be denied,
The scars will show and tell
That self-inflicted wounds
Have not been healing well.

MARTIN LUTHER

Struck down on the road to somewhere
He shook like a leaf
And gathered in a moment
The ordering principles of a new life In the real world.

But as a monk he now felt things
Un-monkish at best.
Concepts fell into place,
And he soon looked with sympathy
On the dear, drab brothers.

But in that long look
His eyes also came to light
On a heavy, plated thing,
Chained to an ancient wooden stand.
A second bolt cracked the heavy tree.

Luther laughed like a madman
For what he saw beckoning
Was the Word of the Living God,
And he suddenly knew
It was rich, uninterpreted, and fallow.

Martin Luther (1483–1546), seminal figure in the Protestant Reformation

LIAISON

Indecently exposed,
A dangling cigarette.
The mouth—is it a tease,
A pout, or is it fret?

The time you have to leave,
The hardest time of all.
You nod your head and pass
The stranger in the hall.

REMEMBERING

I remember being happy,
I remember being glad.
Far above my fellow creatures,
O, the riches that I had.

Life went down its list of prospects,
Those for sorrow, those for tears.
Now the life I long remember
Calls retreat, then disappears.

LITTLE FINGERS, LITTLE TOES

Little fingers, little toes,
That is how the baby goes.
Crawling here and crawling there,
Crawling almost everywhere.

Bee sting ankles, bee sting knees,
Baby walking now on these.
Running faster that he should.
Running fast will do him good.

Muscled biceps, chunky thighs,
O, how quick the sweetness flies.
New demands are crowding in
Turning babies into men.

Nothing better than to stand
Straight, erect, a healthy man.
Looking outward every day,
Putting childhood things away.

Wisdom whispers, "Not so fast!
Let the precious moments last.
Soon enough to be full grown.
You will harvest what you've sown."

Age is age and youth is youth,
And the learning of the truth
Only comes by going where
Life itself is waiting there.

Unrequited love thrown in,
And the agonies of sin,
Make the man to wish he had
Stayed much longer as a lad.

Little fingers, little toes—
O, how fast the baby grows.
Though unseen, my dearest one,
Time is watching as you run.

THE SCOTTSBORO BOYS

"Dem Brothers done raped us!"
    And the Scottsboro boys
    Went down, Moses.
Who did you tap
    To turn those shotguns into snakes,
    To send down murrain
    On the rich, red beef?
Who did you send
    To tell those hot-pants girls,
    "You got it vice versa'd,
    Don't ya know?"

Nine African-American men wrongly accused of sexual assault in 1931

THE WALDENSIAN

It was more than a matter of bettering myself.
I know that my language was rough
And my ways were crude.
I had no interest in wealth
And it was more than a matter of food.
When they spoke of all this
In the church in my village
I cannot describe the ways that I felt.
We debated and worshipped, and as I knelt,
It was certain! I would come—not to pillage
Or rule, or replace anyone, just to live.
I left behind a heritage and history, mine,
And all of ours. That was hard.
But we did hope that our reward
Would be in what we'd find.
Sometimes we were disappointed, sometimes not.
I am an American now, like everyone else here.
I would not go back.
For what? A wretched tract
Of land, and though I might love it,
I fear it would not serve me like this valley has.
The first time I saw it the sun
Was brighter than on most days.
The air was warm, the trees rich
And green, flashing in the rays.
The train stopped with a sudden, grinding jolt,
And I stepped off in my anxious boldness.

A religious group of southern Europeans who settled in North Carolina in the late 1800's

RETURN

I am returning to you
After a week of parting,
In which time you have never done wrong.
And I have watched the monument
I was building so carefully, so deliberately.
If it is false and reactive
To a man's need for his place,
It is not altogether useless,
For what I idolize in you,
I am happy to discover,
Are the gifts you give to an ordinary day.
They are precious, and I am rushing
To hoard them like rare jewels.
Woman, be proud!
There is wisdom growing in these stiff bones.

ELEGY

Rest now upon the waving lap of earth.
As we see about us a carpet for your play,
We must accept your passing.
We can dream of your sleep
Among this wind—blown grass.
We embrace your living on, here,
In this soft, eternal motion.

This is a place for you,
Who never saw it, nor walked nearby.
But knowing you, we choose it,
And lay you down as gently
As strong men can be gentle.
Be no stranger here, child,
For you are home.
Welcome us when we come.

THEY HAVE THEIR REWARD

And they shall be rewarded for their help,
For the hours of long endurance,
For wearing strength and courage like the sun.
And they shall be rewarded for their help.

And they shall be rewarded for their peace,
That nourished their convictions like the soil,
That blossomed through their weeping like a flower.
And they shall be rewarded for that peace.

And they shall be rewarded for their care.
Not fluids of suffering bodies, nor their wastes,
Nor screams, nor death itself could keep them back.
They shall be so rewarded for their care.

And they shall be rewarded for their faith,
That though they hurt and writhed they would be eased,
That though they died unhealed they would not die.
They then have their rewarding for that faith.

I think that their reward shall be to sense
That lost ones live above the plane of time.
The intuition is the difference.
I think that their reward shall be to climb.

UNIVERSALISM

"God . . . is the Savior of all . . ." 1 Timothy 4:10

They laughed in mockery and scorn
When I stood up to preach.
I took them in so graciously;
I have eternal reach.

WHAT FINGERS CANNOT HOLD

What fingers cannot hold
Can still be held in heart.
A lightness it can be
And on the air depart.

But I will tell you this—
In all the world around
What some hold in the heart
Would bring the mighty down.

IN THE BEGINNING . . .

And on the 8th day, God said,
"Let there be poetry,"
And behold there was poetry.
And God saw it and said
"It is very good.
Now, let poetry find a poet."
And it has been the Eighth Day ever since.

SWIMMING IN THE LAKE OF FIRE

"... the place for them is the lake burning with fire and sulphur ..."
    Revelation 21: 8

It is eternity's best subterfuge,
This Resurrection by the Crystal Sea.
Eternal life within their fingertips!
The drowning learn it is not meant to be.

Somnambulant in coffin's best attire,
They shuffle toward the vast, inviting Lake,
Oblivious of those who disappear,
And to the sucking sounds the waters make.

They flounder first who were not taught to swim,
Down to the scalding hydrothermal vents,
Once thought to be the origin of life,
But from this place no more unique ascents.

Imperially, God sits on the Throne.
The struggling ones can view the holy sight—
The author of this brilliant camouflage,
Who flicks his gnarling fingers left or right.

The end of everything—this is the End!
No trumpet-blaring angel, not a sound.
Not one returning to the Peaceful Shore—
The arms grow flaccid, and they all go down.

ESKIMO SURVIVAL

It is an extremely loving thing
To chew the meat to such
A fine consistency
That you can pass it on the tongue
To the mouth of mother
Who has no teeth.
Thus, you are sure,
She will live on,
To teach your children and theirs,
Until the sustenance of such love
Is not quite enough.

AT NAGS HEAD

At these sand mounds you flew the world,
And fired the fantastic flight
Of gigantic things of pleasure, war, and dare.
You launched an age's small and timid mind
Into the realms of birds, clouds, space,
And set a lover's moon in every eye.
I have wondered at your information,
At the world without such galactic facts.
Yet, on that December day
You presented your ambiguous achievement.
Sand, gulls, air, ideas scattered in your rattling path.
Even God was aghast when your blithe glider
Took wind and flew.

Site of the Wright Brothers' first flight, 1903

TO MY FATHER

I had forgiven you
And was determined to be reconciled.
    In my preparation,
        You died.
I forgive you for dying
And tell you, wherever you are:
    We are reconciled.
    I am your son, come home.
You did not put me
    Under the awful burden
    Of having a perfect father.
Nor did I so burden you.

THOMAS RONALD VAUGHAN is a poet and writer from the American South. Both sets of grandparents were farmers in rural Virginia, and he has lived in five Southern states.

Vocationally, he was a healthcare administrator and a parish minister in two mainline Protestant denominations. His publications include *A Second Circle in the Dust*; *The Love of God and the Age to Come: No Eternal Hell*; *God and The Twelve Problems of Evil: Into Great Mystery*; and *Being Deaf at the Tower of Babel: Poems*.

He and his wife, Jayne, live in the mountains of western North Carolina.

www.ingramcontent.com/pod-product-compliance
Lightning Source LLC
Chambersburg PA
CBHW061503040426
42450CB00008B/1467